RISING STARS ASSESSING PROGRESS

USING AND APPLYING MATHEMATICS SKILLS

Tasks to support Assessment for Learning

YEAR 3

Louise Moore and Pamela Wyllie

Rising Stars UK Ltd, 22 Grafton Street, London W1S 4EX

www.risingstars-uk.com

All facts are correct at time of going to press.

Published 2009
Reprinted 2010

Text, design and layout © 2009 Rising Stars UK Ltd.

Design and Illustrations: Redmoor Design, Tavistock, Devon
Cover design: Burville-Riley Partnership

Rising Stars is grateful to the following people who have
contributed to the development of these materials:
Mathematics consultant: Alan Parr
Publishing consultant: Lindsey Charles

We are grateful to the following schools for helping us to develop
this edition:
Aisling Begley, St Nicholas Primary School, Oxford
Judith Standing, Holy Trinity Primary School, London

Every effort has been made to trace copyright holders and obtain
their permission for the use of copyright materials. The authors and
publisher will gladly receive information enabling them to rectify
any error or omission in subsequent editions.

All rights reserved. No part of this publication may be reproduced,
stored in a retrieval system, or transmitted, in any form by any
means, electronic, mechanical, photocopying, recording or
otherwise, without the prior permission of Rising Stars.

British Library Cataloguing in Publication Data.
A CIP record for this book is available from the British Library.

ISBN: 978-1-84680-618-6

PEFC
PEFC/16-33-366
Printed by Ashford Colour Press Ltd

CONTENTS

Introduction	4
Task: 'V'ery puzzling	8
Task: Blank puzzles	11
Task: Jump to it!	14
Task: Be square	17
Task: Reflect on this	20
Task: A right 't'angle	23
Task: The YES – NO puzzle	26
Task: Put your foot down!	29
Task: Pathway puzzle	32
Task: Time teaser	35
Task: Sentence seekers	38
Task: Animal magic!	41
My progress and targets sheet	44
Solutions	45

YEAR 3

INTRODUCTION

The *Assessing Progress: Using and Applying Mathematics Skills* series spans years 1 to 6 and has been designed to support Assessing Pupils' Progress (APP) within the structure of the new Primary Framework for mathematics.

For each year there is:

- a photocopiable book with 12 tasks organised by Blocks of the Framework plus full teacher and assessment guidance
- a CD-ROM with all book content in PDF format, an editable version of each pupil task sheet and printable resource sheets for tasks requiring template material.

Using the tasks

The tasks have been developed specifically for use with Framework-based schemes of work. There are two or three tasks for each Block and there are enough tasks for two per half term. The evidence gathered from these can be used in periodic reviews for APP. See page 7 for a full list of tasks and how they relate to the Framework Blocks.

The tasks are accessible to children working in a range of National Curriculum levels and differentiation is usually by outcome, allowing children to demonstrate the highest attainment they can. In some tasks, different resources are suggested that may be used by children working at lower levels if necessary.

Children may work on the tasks individually, in pairs or in groups. We recommend that the task is introduced through class or group discussion to ensure that all children understand what is expected, especially if they have English as an additional language.

Using mathematical language

The mathematical language used in the tasks follows the guidance in the Strategy's *Mathematical vocabulary* about the terminology which should be introduced in each year. Further help with vocabulary for teachers can be found in the QCA's *Mathematics glossary for teachers in key stages 1-4* at http://www.qca.org.uk/qca_6922.aspx.

Gathering and using evidence for APP

Each task has assessment guidance for the teacher, which shows how possible outcomes relate to National Curriculum levels and APP assessment focuses (AFs) for Ma1* Using and applying mathematics: problem solving; communicating; and reasoning. (See 'What's in a task?' below for further information.) This makes it easy to relate task outcomes directly to children's APP assessment guidelines.

The assessment guidance in each pack covers the range of levels at which the majority of children are working in that year group. See the table below for a summary. (Children working below or above these level ranges could be given tasks from the book for the year below or above.)

Year 1	Year 2	Year 3	Year 4	Year 5	Year 6
Levels 1–2	Levels 1–3	Levels 2–3	Levels 2–4	Levels 3–4	Levels 3–5

* Note that attainment target Ma1 is likely to be changed to Mathematical processes and applications in autumn 2009 in order to bring terminology in line with the secondary curriculum. Proposals had not been confirmed at the time of going to press.

YEAR 3 INTRODUCTION

Task outcomes provide good evidence for assessment purposes. The outcomes may be children's written work, or their verbal feedback to the teacher or teaching assistant. When circulating during the task, teachers and teaching assistants will see what children do and hear their reasoning and these observations can also provide useful evidence.

Note that for Key Stage 1, children's responses are less likely to be written and more of the evidence for assessment will be observational. Children may also take photographs, e.g. of models they have made. They may use technology, e.g. printing out their work using ICT or making a video recording of a special presentation.

Target sheets for pupils

'My progress and targets' sheets are supplied for children to fill in or update either after each task or after a number of tasks.

Further teacher support

Details of the possible mathematical outcomes of the tasks (or solutions), as opposed to the skills outcomes, are provided on pages 45–48. Additional material, such as an example spreadsheet, is provided on the CD-ROM where appropriate.

What's in a task?

Each task has the following components:

- Pupil sheet
- Teacher notes on running the task, outcomes and Framework references
- APP assessment guidance

The pupil sheet

- The problem and **Your task**: introduces the problem for children to solve in a scenario.
- **Think about**: focuses children's attention on aspects of the task
- **For the puzzle book**: an optional mini-extension to the main task. Children can build up a puzzle book throughout the year, in groups or as a class. It is a good way of reviewing and building on the tasks and supplies further activities for children who finish quickly. It also provides a record of their maths work which children can share with their parents or carers.
- An editable version of each task is provided on the CD-ROM. The text can be adapted to meet the needs of children. Note, however, that the formatting may change from the original.

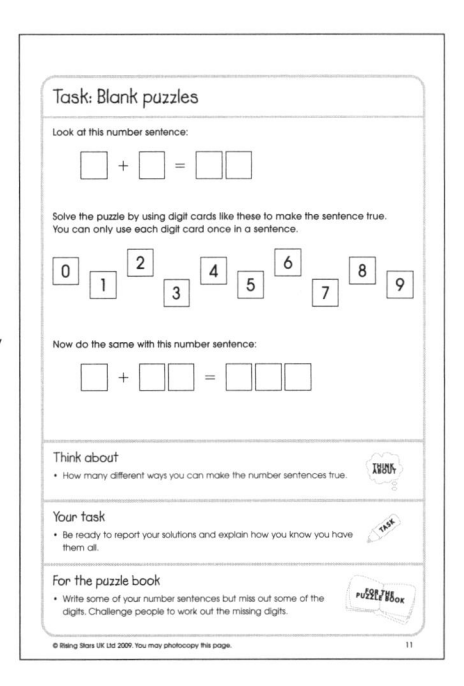

INTRODUCTION

YEAR 3

The teacher notes

- **Framework**: shows where the task fits within the Framework Blocks and Units. The complete wording of the relevant Framework learning objective is provided. Where aspects are not covered by a task, that part of the objective is shown in a light tint.

- **Materials**: lists all materials which may be needed for the task. Children can choose what they use so not all the material prepared may be needed. Details of any template resource sheets provided on the CD-ROM are given in this section.

- **Getting started**: describes some ways to start the task and additional guidance to give children verbally, e.g. a reminder to think about how to record the shapes they make.

- **What might happen during the task**: indicates what may happen during the task and can be referred to while circulating among groups as they work. These are examples of typical responses, not a comprehensive list. If children are struggling, however, these may also prove useful prompts. They can also be used as the basis for questions to gain insight into children's thinking (see **What to look for** section also).

Assessment guidance

- The table shows what the outcomes from the task might look like for different assessment focuses and levels. The text in italics provides examples of ways that children typically demonstrate the mathematics used in the task.

- The guidance mirrors the organisation of the APP guidelines published by the National Strategies. This means that evidence from the task can be related easily to APP assessment guidelines.

- **Extension and related activities**: includes suggestions for further teaching of the skills and processes of using and applying mathematics. They are designed for use in a lesson after children have completed the task on the pupil sheet. Each extension activity could take at least one lesson and could be used, alternatively, as a further assessment opportunity later in the term or year.

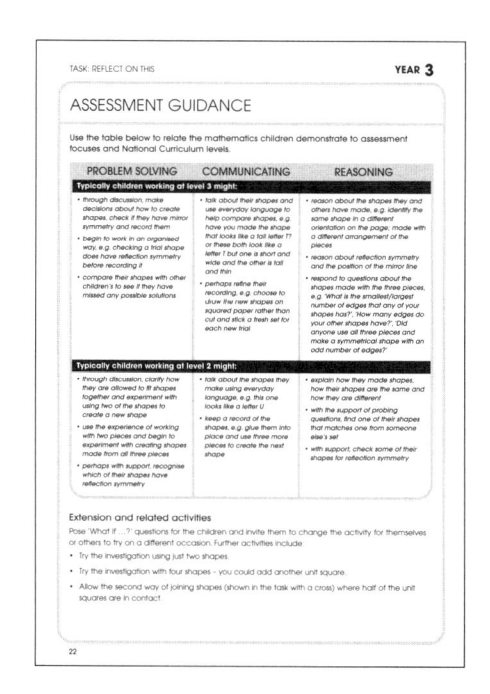

YEAR 3

INTRODUCTION

My progress and targets sheet

- Present APP criteria in pupil-friendly language*.
- Enable children to summarise what they feel they can do.
- Encourage children to write their own targets.
- Can be used after each task or after a number of tasks.
- Present criteria that relate to two levels per sheet to prevent it being overwhelming or intimidating. The lower level is always shown in the bottom row of the table.

Information about the levels covered on each sheet is included in the footer on the page. For example, the sheet for level 2–3 is labelled 'L2/3'. The information is for the teacher. Each level describes about two years of mathematical development and children's progress can be thought of in terms of increasing depth within a level as well as movement from one level to the next. For these reasons we have not made the level information more prominent for children to read.

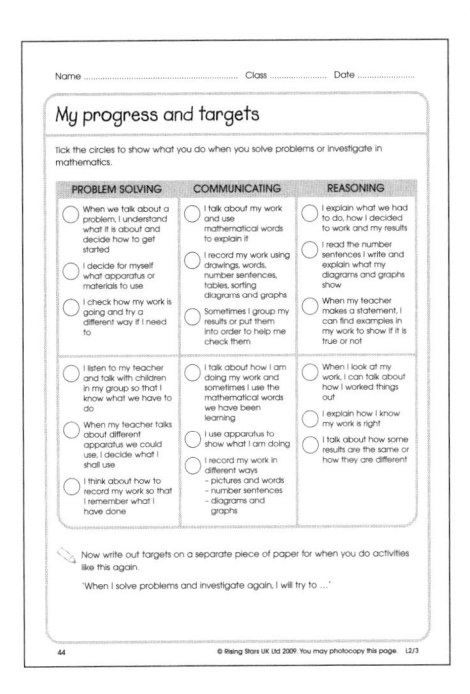

Tasks for Year 3 and how they relate to the Framework

Task	Framework reference
'V'ery puzzling	Block A: Counting, partitioning and calculating, Unit 1
Blank puzzles	Block A: Counting, partitioning and calculating, Units 1, 2 and 3
Jump to it!	Block A: Counting, partitioning and calculating, Units 1, 2 and 3
Be square	Block B: Securing number facts, understanding shapes, Units 1, 2 and 3
Reflect on this	Block B: Securing number facts, understanding shapes, Units 1, 2 and 3
A right 't'angle	Block B: Securing number facts, understanding shapes, Unit 3
The YES – NO puzzle	Block C: Handling data and measures, Units 1 and 2
Put your foot down!	Block C: Handling data and measures, Units 1, 2 and 3
Pathway puzzle	Block D: Calculating, measuring and understanding shape, Units 1 and 2
Time teaser	Block D: Calculating, measuring and understanding shape, Units 1 and 3
Sentence seekers	Block E: Securing number facts, relationships and calculating, Units 1, 2 and 3
Animal magic!	Block E: Securing number facts, relationships and calculating, Units 2 and 3

* Completing the sheets should be as meaningful as possible for children. We recommend that teachers talk through the statements with children so that they understand the sometimes quite subtle differences between statements below and above the line. Children should also be talking through their personal targets with the teacher so that the targets are appropriate and likely to have some impact on their mathematical development.

7

Task: 'V'ery puzzling

Give each side of the 'V' the same total.

Solve this puzzle by putting digit cards like these into the boxes. You can only use each digit card once.

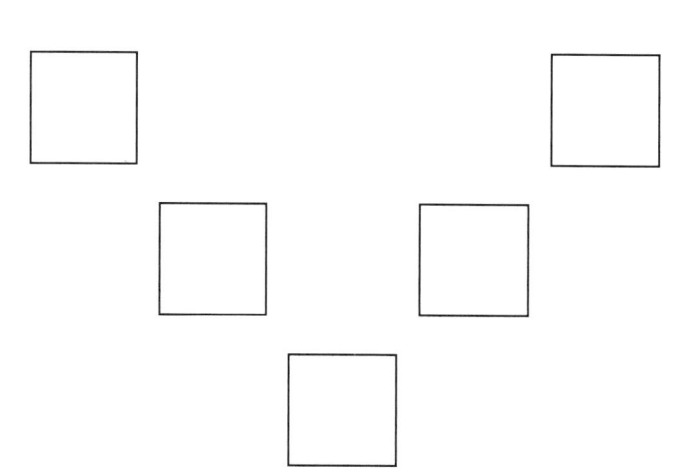

Think about
- How many different ways can you put the numbers in the boxes so each side has the same total?

Your task
- Find all the ways you can to put the numbers in the boxes so that each side has the same total.
- Be ready to convince other people you have all of the ways.

For the puzzle book
- Draw one of your solutions but leave three of the cards blank. Challenge people to work out the missing cards.

© Rising Stars UK Ltd 2009. You may photocopy this page.

YEAR 3

TASK: 'V'ERY PUZZLING

TEACHER NOTES

Framework: Year 3 Block A: Counting, partitioning and calculating

Unit 1: Derive and recall all addition and subtraction facts for each number to 20, sums and differences of multiples of 10 and number pairs that total 100

Materials
- A set of digit cards 1–5 for each child

Getting started
- Ask the children how they might get started.
- Leave as many decisions as possible to individual children:
  - whether the number order on the sides matters or not.
- Check that the children have a way of getting started:
  - you might ask one or two children to place their digit cards in the 'V' and find the totals of the sides.

What might happen during the task
- Children decide for themselves how to record their successful (and maybe their unsuccessful) attempts:
  - copying the 'V' formation of the digit cards they have arranged
  - listing the number order from left to right
  - writing a list of the numbers on each arm of the 'V'.
- They may begin to be systematic in the way they try the digit cards in different positions:
  - try all the possible arrangements with 1 at the base of the 'V', then 2 etc.
  - start with 1 at the start of the first side and find all the possible arrangements.
- They decide whether they have found all the possible solutions and demonstrate different degrees of mathematical reasoning:
  - that must be all because I can't find any more
  - I compared my answers to everyone's in the group and no one had a different answer
  - I tried every number at the bottom of the 'V' so there aren't any other ways to do it.
- They explain patterns in solutions and demonstrate different degrees of mathematical reasoning:
  - these are all the ways to put the digit cards so that the sides of the 'V' have the same total
  - the ones that work all have an odd number at the bottom of the 'V'
  - when there's an odd number at the bottom of the 'V', that leaves an odd and an even number for each side and you can always make two pairs with the same total
  - there are three odd numbers and two even numbers and that's an odd number for the bottom and an odd and an even for each edge.
- If a child is stuck, you might ask a question or prompt them to review what they have done so far:
  - how did you decide to start?
  - tell me what you have found so far
  - can you see anything the same about the ones that do/don't work?
- Encourage the children to draw conclusions from their activity by talking or writing about what they have found.

What to look for
- Look for what children say and do, as well as what they record.
- Ask questions about the work to gain insights into their thinking.

TASK: 'V'ERY PUZZLING

YEAR **3**

ASSESSMENT GUIDANCE

Use the table below to relate the mathematics children demonstrate to assessment focuses and National Curriculum levels.

PROBLEM SOLVING	COMMUNICATING	REASONING
Typically children working at level 3 might:		
• begin to create different arrangements in a more organised way • check an arrangement gives the same total along each side of the 'V' before recording it • begin to check results to see if any recorded arrangements are the same	• decide how to record results, perhaps refining the approach to be less time consuming • interpret other children's recording to compare results	• explain their 'rule' for deciding if two arrangements are the same or not • review their work and explain their approach to creating different, successful arrangements • notice that all successful arrangements have an odd number at the base of the 'V' and another odd and an even number on either side of it
Typically children working at level 2 might:		
• engage with the activity in a practical way, e.g. arrange digit cards and add the numbers along each side of the 'V' • try different arrangements of digit cards to see if both sides of the 'V' have the same total	• talk about the arrangements they make and the totals they find • begin to record their arrangements to remember what they have tried so far • decide how to record results, e.g. decide to draw boxes in a 'V' formation to represent digit cards and write the numbers in them	• identify arrangements that resulted in each side having the same total • talk about how two arrangements are the same or differ, e.g. these have the same numbers at the bottom of the 'V' but the other numbers aren't in the same order • identify arrangements that have the same 'side total'

Extension and related activities

Pose 'What if ...?' questions for the children and invite them to change the activity for others to try on a different occasion. Further activities include:

- Make a larger 'V' and use digit cards 1–7.
- Use an 'X' or 'Y' instead of a 'V'.
- Use digit cards with a different set of consecutive numbers, e.g. 8, 9, 10, 11, 12.
- Use a set of consecutive even numbers, e.g. 2, 4, 6, 8, 10.

Task: Blank puzzles

Look at this number sentence:

$$\square + \square = \square\square$$

Solve the puzzle by using digit cards like these to make the sentence true. You can only use each digit card once in a sentence.

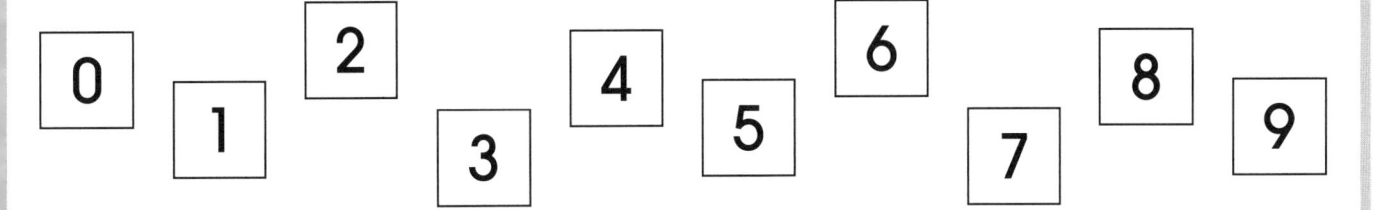

0 1 2 3 4 5 6 7 8 9

Now do the same with this number sentence:

$$\square + \square\square = \square\square\square$$

Think about
- How many different ways you can make the number sentences true.

Your task
- Be ready to report your solutions and explain how you know you have them all.

For the puzzle book
- Write some of your number sentences but miss out some of the digits. Challenge people to work out the missing digits.

© Rising Stars UK Ltd 2009. You may photocopy this page.

TASK: BLANK PUZZLES

YEAR 3

TEACHER NOTES

Framework: Year 3 Block A: Counting Partitioning and calculating

Units 1, 2 and 3: Add or subtract mentally combinations of one-digit and two-digit numbers

Materials
- A set of digit cards 0–9 for each child

Getting started
- Ask the children how they might get started.
- Leave as many decisions as possible to individual children or groups:
  - whether the number order matters, i.e. whether to count $8 + 9 = 17$ and $9 + 8 = 17$ as two different solutions
  - whether the 0 can be a place holder in the tens position on the first sentence, to give totals such as 03, or in the hundreds position in the second sentence.
- Check that the children have a way of getting started:
  - you might ask one or two to create and read a number sentence using the digit cards.

What might happen during the task
- Children decide for themselves how to record their successful attempts.
- They may begin to be systematic in the way they position the digit cards:
  - try all the possible arrangements with 1 in the first box, then 2 etc.
  - use two digits to form an answer and then find all the ways to make that total.
- They decide whether they have found all the possible solutions and demonstrate different degrees of mathematical reasoning:
  - that must be all because I can't find any more
  - I compared my answers to everyone's in the group and no one had a different answer
  - I put 9 in the first box and then tried all the other numbers in the other box to find totals where the answers were two-digit numbers, then I tried 8, then 7 etc.
- If a child is stuck, you might ask a question or prompt them to review what they have done so far:
  - how did you decide to start?
  - tell me what you have found so far
  - you started with a 3 in the first box. Do you have any numbers that you could add to it to make a two-digit total?
- Encourage the children to draw conclusions from each part of their activity by talking or writing about what they have found.

What to look for
- Look for what children say and do, as well as what they record.
- Ask questions about the work to gain insights into their thinking.

YEAR 3

TASK: BLANK PUZZLES

ASSESSMENT GUIDANCE

Use the table below to relate the mathematics children demonstrate to assessment focuses and National Curriculum levels.

PROBLEM SOLVING	COMMUNICATING	REASONING
Typically children working at level 3 might:		
• make decisions, e.g. decide whether to treat 9 + 6 and 6 + 9 as the same solution or not • begin to create different addition sentences in a more organised way, e.g. begin with 5 + 7 = 12 and then try adding other numbers to 5	• record their addition sentences so that they can check their results • refer to their recording to talk about the addition sentences they made and their conclusions	• use the addition facts they know and reason about their results, e.g. explain how they know that 17 is the largest two-digit total they can make; recognise that the two-digit number must be '90-something' if adding a single-digit number is to result in a three-digit total • review their work and reason about how they know they have all possible solutions
Typically children working at level 2 might:		
• engage with the activity in a practical way, e.g. choose pairs of single-digit numbers to add and check that they have digit cards available to show the two-digit total • begin to use the addition facts to 10 that they know to help choose pairs of single-digit numbers • remember the 'rules' of the activity, e.g. that each digit card can be used only once in any sentence and that an addition such as 9 + 2 = 11 is not allowed	• talk about their choice of digit cards to add and the totals they make • record their addition sentences so that they can use the digit cards again in another sentence	• begin to compare results with others and talk about whether two recorded results are the same or different • use the results of their trial additions to help them choose another appropriate pair of numbers to add, e.g. record 9 + 6 = 15 and reason that the total of 9 + 7 will be one more

Extension and related activities

Pose 'What if …?' questions for the children and invite them to change the activity for others to try on a different occasion. Further activities include:

- Try TU + U = TU.
- Allow two sets of digit cards so children can use more than one of each digit.
- Only allow even number answers.

Task: Jump to it!

Children in Class A are using a number track to make sequences.

Each time they start on 0 and make jumps of different sizes.

Leah makes a number sequence by starting on 0 and jumping along three at a time. What is her sequence?

Isaac makes different sequences that include the number 20. He starts on 0 and decides how big to make the jumps.

Think about

- Where you must start.
- How big to make each jump.
- Which number you must remember to land on.

Your task

- Find sequences that start at 0 and contain the number 20 *and* the number 50.
- Find as many different sequences as you can.

For the puzzle book

- Make some other sequences that start on 0 and have different jump sizes. Choose one of your sequences. Tell people the start number and two of the numbers that are in your sequence. Challenge people to find the sequence that starts on the number you chose and includes both of the other numbers. Remember to make sure that your sequence is correct and check if there is more than one solution!

YEAR 3

TASK: JUMP TO IT!

TEACHER NOTES

Framework: Year 3 Block A: Counting, partitioning and calculating

Units 1, 2 and 3: Read, write and order whole numbers to at least 1000 and position them on a number line; count on from and back to zero in single-digit steps or multiples of 10

Materials

- A number track or number line on the classroom floor, or chalked onto the playground surface
- Other number lines or tracks to 100

Getting started

- Ask the children how they might get started.
- Leave as many decisions as possible to individual children:
  - the size of jump
  - how to record their work.
- Check that the children have a way of getting started:
  - using a number track on the classroom floor or in the playground, you might ask children to make Leah's sequence, starting at 0 and jumping in steps of three
  - you might ask children to make sequences that land on the number 4 and see how many they find.

What might happen during the task

- Children decide for themselves how to record their findings:
  - writing the sequences out
  - making a table of the start number (which should always be 0), jump size and numbers on which they land (circling target numbers).
- They may be systematic in the way they investigate the sequences:
  - find all the possible solutions by increasing the jump size by one each time.
- They explain their findings and demonstrate different degrees of mathematical understanding:
  - if I jump in fives from 0, I land on 20 and 50

  - 20 and 50 are in the 2, 5 and 10 times tables so those size jumps will work if you start on 0.
- If a child is stuck, you might ask a question or prompt them to review what they have done so far:
  - how did you decide to start?
  - how did you make that sequence?
  - what other jump size could you try?
  - are there number facts you already know that could help you?
- Encourage the children to draw conclusions from their activity by talking or writing about what they have found.

What to look for

- Look for what children say and do, as well as what they record.
- Ask questions about the work to gain insights into their thinking.

TASK: JUMP TO IT! YEAR **3**

ASSESSMENT GUIDANCE

Use the table below to relate the mathematics children demonstrate to assessment focuses and National Curriculum levels.

PROBLEM SOLVING	COMMUNICATING	REASONING
Typically children working at level 3 might:		
• adopt a practical approach, jumping a counter along a number track • through discussion, agree how to record the sequences they try • begin to work in an organised way, e.g. checking they have tried steps of two, three, four … • recognise this as a 'counting on' activity and perhaps work on their fingers rather than using a track	• talk about the sequences they have tried, the start numbers and jump sizes • compare their sequences with another child's, interpreting their way of recording and recognising if sequences are the same or different	• explain how they generated their sequences, identifying the step size for each, and how they know they are correct • identify Isaac's sequences, i.e. those that contain 20 • identify all of the sequences that contain 20 and 50 • with the support of probing questions, identify a pair of numbers that both appear in only one sequence, such as 7 and 21
Typically children working at level 2 might:		
• through discussion, agree a practical approach such as working in pairs, e.g. one person chooses a jump size, starts at 0 and jumps a counter along a number track, the partner records the numbers they land on, including the start number 0; partners swap roles • perhaps with prompting, they check their sequences – that each starts at 0, each has a consistent jump size and that the numbers are recorded accurately	• talk about their sequences, the jump sizes they have tried, etc. • take turns to record each sequence, perhaps enclosing each number in a square to represent regions on the number track	• talk about what they have done and how they checked their sequences • look at their sequences and identify the jump sizes • with the support of probing questions, identify different sequences that contain 20 • with further support, identify sequences that contain 20 and 50

Extension and related activities

Pose 'What if …?' questions for the children and invite them to change the activity for others to try on a different occasion. Further activities include:

- Relate the sequences to multiplication, e.g. relate jumps of five from 0 to multiplication facts for five.
- Make sequences with three target numbers.
- Create sequences where the jump size alternates between two values, e.g. begin at 0 and add two, add one, add two, add one … to produce sequences such as 2, 3, 5, 6, 8 …

Task: Be square

Fold a piece of plain paper in half.

Try to make a square by cutting a shape like this out of the paper:

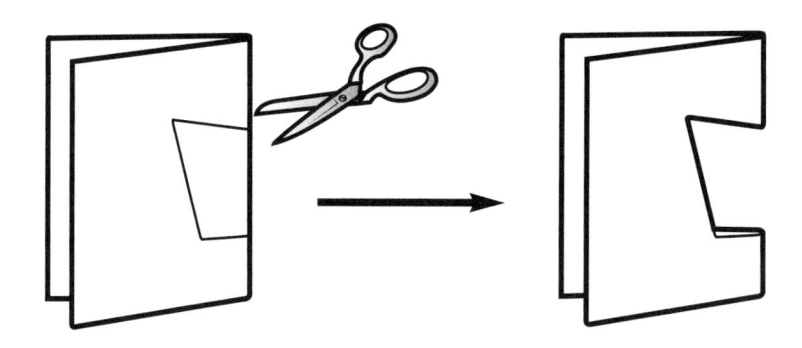

Open up the sheet. Did you make a square hole in the paper? If not, try again!

How many ways can you find to cut a shape so a square hole is left?

What other shapes can you make by cutting along the fold in the paper?

Think about

- How many edges the shape you want to make has, and how many edges the shape you cut needs to have.
- How long the edges need to be.

Your task

- Make different shapes and be ready to describe and discuss how you made them.

For the puzzle book

- Draw a folded piece of paper with the shape you cut drawn onto it. Challenge people to say what shape the hole in the paper will be when you open it out.

© Rising Stars UK Ltd 2009. You may photocopy this page.

TASK: BE SQUARE

YEAR 3

TEACHER NOTES

Framework: Year 3 Block B: Securing number facts, understanding shape

Units 1, 2 and 3: Relate 2-D shapes and 3-D solids to drawings of them; describe, visualise, classify, draw and make the shapes

Materials
- Pieces of paper for children to fold and cut
- Scissors
- Glue

Getting started
- Ask the children how they might get started.
- Leave as many decisions as possible to individual children:
  - what type of shape to cut
  - how to record their work.
- Check that the children have a way of getting started:
  - you might ask them to fold the paper and draw the first shape they are going to cut.

What might happen during the task
- Children decide for themselves how to record their shapes:
  - sticking down the cut shapes or the paper they were cut from
  - drawing the shapes they create
  - making a table of the number of edges on the shape they cut and the number of edges on the hole left in the paper.
- They may be systematic in the way they change the number of cuts:
  - find all the possible shapes with two cuts, then three etc.
  - make a list of polygons and then create them.
- They explain their findings and demonstrate different degrees of mathematical understanding:
  - there are always more edges on the shape than I cut
  - sometimes there are double the number of edges on the shape than I cut
  - I can only make a triangle by cutting out a triangle
  - for shapes with an even number of edges, I can make half the number of cuts as there are edges, as long as I don't start or end at a right angle to the fold
  - for polygons with an odd number of edges, I have to make just over half the number of cuts as there are edges, and I must start or end at a right angle to the fold.
- If a child is stuck, you might ask a question or prompt them to review what they have done so far:
  - how did you decide to start?
  - show me the shapes you have made so far
  - show me a different shape that you could try cutting out.
- Encourage the children to draw conclusions from their activity by talking or writing about what they have found.

What to look for
- Look for what children say and do, as well as what they record.
- Ask questions about the work to gain insights into their thinking.

YEAR 3

TASK: BE SQUARE

ASSESSMENT GUIDANCE

Use the table below to relate the mathematics children demonstrate to assessment focuses and National Curriculum levels.

PROBLEM SOLVING	COMMUNICATING	REASONING
Typically children working at level 3 might:		
• look for more than one way to make the cuts for a square • set their own challenges, e.g. look for different ways to make the cuts to get a shape with three straight edges, five straight edges, a quadrilateral that is not a square etc.	• keep the shapes they cut out and begin to group them, e.g. put all of the hexagons together • talk about different ways to make the cuts to produce a triangle, a shape with four edges/quadrilateral, a pentagon etc.	• reason about different ways to fold a square in half and use this reasoning when they consider the different shapes to cut on the folded paper • recognise that if they make a cut at right angles to the folded edge then that will create one straight edge on the finished shape • reason about the number of cuts and the number of edges on the shape produced
Typically children working at level 2 might:		
• experiment with making straight-line cuts from the folded edge and back to it • use trial and improvement to create a reasonable approximation to a square • create a range of shapes	• keep the shapes they cut out as their record • talk about the shapes using mathematical language, such as 'edge', and using the names of familiar shapes	• reason about the shapes they cut out, e.g. recognise that they are folded in half • begin to reason about the shape they must cut to create a square, e.g. this is nearly right but these cuts must be shorter; on the folded paper it will look like half of a square

Extension and related activities

Pose 'What if …?' questions for the children and invite them to change the activity for themselves or others to try on a different occasion. Further activities include:

- Investigate cutting out quadrilaterals.
- Display the folded shapes and ask children to predict what shape they will be when they are opened out.
- Try the activity with the paper folded once across and once down, and where the centre of the paper must be cut away.

Task: Reflect on this

Look at these three shapes:

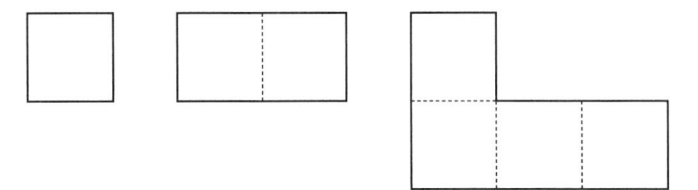

Two of the shapes can be fitted together like this: ✓

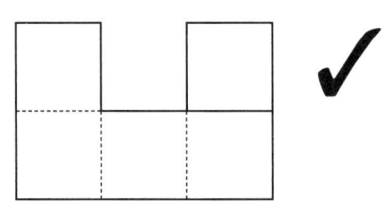

They cannot be fitted together like this: ✗

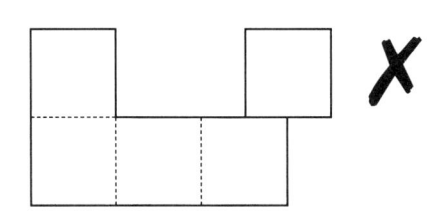

Try fitting two of the shapes together to make different shapes.

Think about

- Whether the shapes you make are symmetrical.
- Any other properties the shapes have.
- The names of the shapes you can make.

Your task

- Find symmetrical shapes by joining all three shapes together. Try to find as many as you can.

For the puzzle book

- Cut a symmetrical shape into three pieces and stick them down separately on a page. Remember to rotate some of the shapes first. Challenge people to work out how to fit them together to make a symmetrical shape.

YEAR 3 TASK: REFLECT ON THIS

TEACHER NOTES

Framework: Year 3 Block B: Securing number facts, understanding shape
Units 1, 2 and 3: Relate 2-D shapes and 3-D solids to drawings of them; describe, visualise, classify, draw and make the shapes
Draw and complete shapes with reflective symmetry; draw the reflection of a shape in a mirror line along one side

Materials
- Cut-outs of the three shapes (or photocopies to be cut out)
- Scissors
- Drawing materials, including squared paper
- Glue
- Mirrors

Getting started
- Ask the children how they might get started.
- Leave as many decisions as possible to individual children:
  - how many shapes to use
  - whether shapes can be flipped over
  - how to record their work.
- Check that the children have a way of getting started:
  - you might ask them to use two of the shapes to make a shape that does not have reflection symmetry and then rearrange them into a shape that does.

What might happen during the task
- Children decide for themselves how to record their findings:
  - drawing the shapes
  - cutting and sticking the pieces.
- They may be systematic in the way they investigate the shapes:
  - keep two shapes fixed in position whilst experimenting with placing the third in different positions around them; then trying again with the first two in a different fixed position
  - checking that an arrangement is not a repeat (although some identical shapes may be created by arranging the three shapes in differently)
  - drawing the mirror line(s) as they record their shapes, to check and demonstrate that the shape is symmetrical
  - organising 'successful' shapes, i.e. those with reflection symmetry, into groups according to the number of edges so that they can check for repeats more easily.
- They explain their findings and demonstrate different degrees of mathematical understanding:
  - I can find a symmetrical shape
  - the shape is the same in the mirror reflection as it is without it so I know it is symmetrical
  - no one in our group found a different one so I think I have them all
  - I know there are no other symmetrical shapes because I have tested each piece in every position.
- If a child is stuck, you might ask a question or prompt them to review what they have done so far:
  - how did you decide to start?
  - how can you check if there are any other shapes?
  - how did you find that symmetrical shape?
  - how can you use the mirror to help you?
- Encourage the children to draw conclusions from their activity by talking or writing about what they have found.

What to look for
- Look for what children say and do, as well as what they record.
- Ask questions about the work to gain insights into their thinking.

TASK: REFLECT ON THIS

YEAR **3**

ASSESSMENT GUIDANCE

Use the table below to relate the mathematics children demonstrate to assessment focuses and National Curriculum levels.

PROBLEM SOLVING	COMMUNICATING	REASONING
Typically children working at level 3 might:		
• through discussion, make decisions about how to create shapes, check if they have mirror symmetry and record them • begin to work in an organised way, e.g. checking a trial shape does have reflection symmetry before recording it • compare their shapes with other children's to see if they have missed any possible solutions	• talk about their shapes and use everyday language to help compare shapes, e.g. have you made the shape that looks like a tall letter T? or these both look like a letter T but one is short and wide and the other is tall and thin • perhaps refine their recording, e.g. choose to draw the new shapes on squared paper rather than cut and stick a fresh set for each new trial	• reason about the shapes they and others have made, e.g. identify the same shape in a different orientation on the page; made with a different arrangement of the pieces • reason about reflection symmetry and the position of the mirror line • respond to questions about the shapes made with the three pieces, e.g. 'What is the smallest/largest number of edges that any of your shapes has?', 'How many edges do your other shapes have?', 'Did anyone use all three pieces and make a symmetrical shape with an odd number of edges?'
Typically children working at level 2 might:		
• through discussion, clarify how they are allowed to fit shapes together and experiment with using two of the shapes to create a new shape • use the experience of working with two pieces and begin to experiment with creating shapes made from all three pieces • perhaps with support, recognise which of their shapes have reflection symmetry	• talk about the shapes they make using everyday language, e.g. this one looks like a letter U • keep a record of the shapes, e.g. glue them into place and use three more pieces to create the next shape	• explain how they made shapes, how their shapes are the same and how they are different • with the support of probing questions, find one of their shapes that matches one from someone else's set • with support, check some of their shapes for reflection symmetry

Extension and related activities

Pose 'What if …?' questions for the children and invite them to change the activity for themselves or others to try on a different occasion. Further activities include:

- Try the investigation using just two shapes.
- Try the investigation with four shapes – you could add another unit square.
- Allow the second way of joining shapes (shown in the task with a cross) where half of the unit squares are in contact.

Task: A right 't'angle

Class 3A are setting shape puzzles for each other.

- Draw a quadrilateral with one right angle and no more.
- Draw a quadrilateral with just two right angles.
- Draw a quadrilateral with exactly three right angles.
- Draw a quadrilateral with four right angles.

Think about
- How can you draw right angles accurately?

Your task
- Draw the quadrilaterals and be ready to describe and discuss how you made them, explaining any problems you had.

For the puzzle book
- Challenge people to draw a named shape with a given number of right angles in it.

© Rising Stars UK Ltd 2009. You may photocopy this page.

TASK: A RIGHT 'T'ANGLE

YEAR 3

TEACHER NOTES

Framework: Year 3 Block B: Securing number facts, understanding shape
Unit 3: Use a set square to draw right angles and to identify right angles in 2-D shapes; compare angles with a right angle; recognise that a straight line is equivalent to two right angles

Materials
- Set squares
- Right-angle measures such as a piece of paper folded twice to create a right angle
- Rulers

Getting started
- Ask the children how they might get started.
- Leave as many decisions as possible to individual children:
  - how many of each type of quadrilateral to draw
  - how to record their work.
- Check that the children have a way of getting started:
  - you might ask them to use the set square to draw their first right angle.

What might happen during the task
- Children decide for themselves how to record their shapes and achieve differing degrees of accuracy.
- They may be systematic in the way they try to develop different quadrilaterals:
  - try the right angles in opposite or adjacent corners.
- They explain their findings and demonstrate different degrees of mathematical understanding:
  - I could make lots of shapes with one right angle
  - I could make a kite with two right angles
  - there isn't a quadrilateral with three right angles because I tried them all
  - if you use three right angles, the other angle is always a right angle as well.

- If a child is stuck, you might ask a question or prompt them to review what they have done so far:
  - how did you decide to start?
  - show me the shapes you have made so far
  - try a quadrilateral with a different number of right angles.
- Encourage the children to draw conclusions from their activity by talking or writing about what they have found.

What to look for
- Look for what children say and do, as well as what they record.
- Ask questions about the work to gain insights into their thinking.

YEAR 3

TASK: A RIGHT 'T'ANGLE

ASSESSMENT GUIDANCE

Use the table below to relate the mathematics children demonstrate to assessment focuses and National Curriculum levels.

PROBLEM SOLVING	COMMUNICATING	REASONING
Typically children working at level 3 might:		
• begin to work in an organised way, e.g. drawing quadrilaterals with only one right angle, exactly two right angles etc. • check the accuracy of their right angles • compare their quadrilaterals with others' drawings to see if there are other possibilities	• begin to organise their recording, e.g. grouping different quadrilaterals with just one right angle, exactly two right angles etc. • begin to use the mathematical convention for labelling the right angles • talk about the quadrilaterals they create and begin to explain their thinking, e.g. when you make three right angles, it automatically turns into four right angles	• reason about quadrilaterals and their properties, e.g. begin to recognise that two right angles can be placed in a quadrilateral next to each other (adjacent) or not (opposite) • conclude that it is not possible to draw a quadrilateral with exactly three right angles • review their work and pose their own challenges, e.g. I've drawn a kite with two right angles. Can you?, I'm going to try a quadrilateral with no right angles
Typically children working at level 2 might:		
• through discussion, clarify what has to be done • use a ruler and set square as shown by the teacher to draw quadrilaterals with different numbers of right angles • use trial and improvement to create a range of quadrilaterals with different numbers of right angles	• draw quadrilaterals • talk about the quadrilaterals they draw using everyday language and some mathematical terms such as 'edge', 'angle', 'right angle', 'same length' • use the names of familiar quadrilaterals	• talk about what is the same about quadrilaterals they draw and how they differ, e.g. they both have four edges but this has one right angle and that has two right angles • recognise that no one has drawn a quadrilateral with exactly three right angles and conclude it may be impossible

Extension and related activities

Pose 'What if ...?' questions for the children and invite them to change the activity for themselves or others to try on a different occasion. Further activities include:

- Investigate different polygons with different numbers of right angles.
- Make some symmetrical polygons that have just one right angle.

Task: The YES – NO puzzle

Look at this sorting diagram:

	multiples of 3	not multiples of 3
multiples of 2		
not multiples of 2		

Work out where these numbers go in the diagram.

| 5 | 8 |

Think about
- How you can check if the numbers are in the right part of the diagram.
- Other numbers that can go in the diagram.

Your task
- Put other correct numbers in the diagram.
- Try to have at least five numbers in each part of it.
- Report on what you notice about the group of numbers in each part of the diagram.

For the puzzle book
- Create and fill in some Carroll diagrams. Remove the headings and see if anyone can work out what they were.

YEAR 3

TASK: THE YES – NO PUZZLE

TEACHER NOTES

Framework: Year 3 Block C: Handling data and measures

Units 1 and 2: Use Venn diagrams or Carroll diagrams to sort data using more than one criterion

Materials

- Have a range of materials from which children can make their own selection:
  - large sheets of paper
  - counting equipment such as cubes
  - number lines
  - calculators.

Getting started

- Ask the children how they might get started.
- Leave as many decisions as possible to individual children:
  - the size of numbers to consider
  - whether to use negative numbers.
- Check that the children have a way of getting started:
  - you might ask one or two to give examples of multiples of a given number.

What might happen during the task

- Children make decisions about whether numbers are multiples of two, three or both.
- They record numbers in the diagram.
- They may be systematic in the way they test numbers:
  - list numbers from one and mark off the multiples of two and three
  - write out the two and three times tables
  - use a calculator to check if a number is a multiple of two, three or both.
- They decide whether their solution is accurate and demonstrate different degrees of mathematical reasoning:
  - they must be right because each part of the diagram has four numbers in it
  - I compared my answers to everyone's in the group and they were all similar
  - I tried the numbers in each part of the diagram and they wouldn't fit anywhere else
  - all the numbers on the top row are even and all the numbers on the bottom are odd
  - all the numbers in the first cell are multiples of six.
- If a child is stuck, you might ask a question or prompt them to review what they have done so far:
  - how did you decide to start?
  - how can you decide where a number fits on the diagram?
  - tell me what you have found so far.
- Encourage the children to draw conclusions from their activity by talking or writing about what they have found.

What to look for

- Look for what children say and do, as well as what they record.
- Ask questions about the work to gain insights into their thinking.

27

TASK: THE YES – NO PUZZLE

YEAR **3**

ASSESSMENT GUIDANCE

Use the table below to relate the mathematics children demonstrate to assessment focuses and National Curriculum levels.

PROBLEM SOLVING	COMMUNICATING	REASONING
Typically children working at level 3 might:		
• use discussion to clarify the task and decide on an approach • suggest different ways to check if a number is a multiple of two or of three and work with larger numbers • choose numbers to sort in a more reasoned way, e.g. use a list of 3× multiplication facts to select even multiples of three for the region 'multiple of two and multiple of three'	• draw and interpret a two-criteria Carroll diagram • refer to their diagram to help explain their thinking • compare diagrams and check other's chosen numbers	• explain how they know that numbers have been placed correctly • say what is the same about numbers in various regions of the diagram, e.g. in the right-hand column as well as in any particular cell • understand the general statement 'all numbers that are multiples of two and of three are also multiples of six' and check examples from their diagrams
Typically children working at level 2 might:		
• through discussion, gain insights into the task, e.g. relate 'is a multiple of two' to a listed 2 × multiplication table or understand it as 'can be made from groups of two cubes' • with the support of group discussion, find a starting point such as writing numbers on cards to move them around the diagram • draw on previous experience of two-criteria Carroll diagrams to make decisions about how to place their chosen numbers correctly	• choose numbers to check and sort in a random way • talk about numbers and how they will know if they are multiples of two or three • draw and label a Carroll diagram using the given model • place number cards or write numbers directly onto the diagram according to their properties	• explain how they checked the properties of a number and how they know they have placed it correctly on the diagram • say what is the same about all of the numbers in one cell of the diagram • begin to use pattern in 2 × multiplication facts to predict which numbers greater than 20 are also multiples of two

Extension and related activities

Pose 'What if …?' questions for the children and invite them to change the activity for themselves or others to try on a different occasion. Further activities include:

- Complete a diagram for multiples of two and four and discuss the results.
- Complete with numbers greater than 100.
- Complete a Venn diagram for the same information and compare the two ways to show the same information, e.g. identify regions that correspond.
- Complete Venn and Carroll diagrams using their own criteria, cover the criterion labels and see if someone can work out what they were.

Task: Put your foot down!

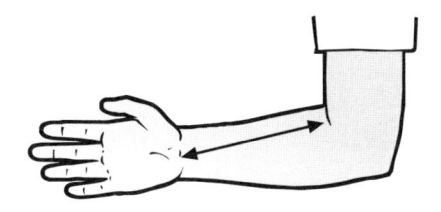

I think your foot is about as long as it is from the crease in your wrist to the crease in your elbow!

But is that true for everyone?

Think about
- How to collect the information you need.
- Which age groups you are going to use.

Your task
- Collect data and use it to decide if the statement is true for everyone.

For the puzzle book
- Use pictures of people and label the length of their arm from the elbow to the wrist. Challenge people to estimate the length of the feet of each person.

TASK: PUT YOUR FOOT DOWN! YEAR 3

TEACHER NOTES

Framework: Year 3 Block C: Handling data and measures

Units 1, 2 and 3: Follow a line of enquiry by deciding what information is important; make and use lists, tables and graphs to organise and interpret the information

Materials

- Have a range of materials from which children can make their own selection:
  - rulers, metre sticks, tape measures (check that children know where to start measuring – the 0 isn't always at the end of measuring equipment!)
  - large sheets of paper
  - scissors
  - glue.

Getting started

- Ask the children how they might get started.

- Leave as many decisions as possible to individual children:
  - where the creases in the wrist and elbow are
  - the sample size
  - the age and height of the sample
  - which resources to use
  - whether to measure or use comparison
  - how accurate the measurement needs to be.

- Check that the children have a way of getting started:
  - you might ask one or two how they are going to compare the lengths.

What might happen during the task

- Children make decisions about whether the lengths are close enough to be considered the same or not.

- They decide for themselves how to record the measurements they have taken:
  - by drawing lines to represent the measurements
  - by drawing round and cutting out the shape of the foot
  - by writing down the measurements
  - by creating a table and writing the measurements in it
  - by recording the difference between the two lengths.

- If a child is stuck, you might ask a question or prompt them to review what they have done so far:
  - how did you decide to start?
  - how can you compare the two measurements?
  - which way do you think is best to measure the lengths?
  - tell me what you have found so far
  - have you measured enough people to find an answer?
  - is your answer true for everybody?

- Encourage the children to draw conclusions from their activity by talking or writing about what they have found.

What to look for

- Look for what children say and do, as well as what they record.

- Ask questions about the work to gain insights into their thinking.

YEAR 3   TASK: PUT YOUR FOOT DOWN!

ASSESSMENT GUIDANCE

Use the table below to relate the mathematics children demonstrate to assessment focuses and National Curriculum levels.

PROBLEM SOLVING	COMMUNICATING	REASONING
Typically children working at level 3 might:		
• discuss how to investigate the situation and agree the information they need to collect • suggest ways to compare and record measurements and, individually or with a partner, decide on an approach • review their work and check that they have the information they need to be able to draw conclusions from their investigation	• record measurements in a way that provides the information they want • refer to their recording to talk about what they have found • begin to use comparative language such as 'longer', 'shorter', 'more people', 'most people'	• review their work and begin to draw conclusions about whether the statement is true for most of the people they have measured: talk about the number of people whose measurements were about the same or whose foot was longer/shorter • respond to questions such as 'What if you tried this with more children?' or 'Do you think this might be true for older children? Why? Why not? How could you find out?'
Typically children working at level 2 might:		
• through group discussion, agree ways to compare measurements and decide which people to measure • talk about how to remember the measurements and agree a way to record them	• record measurements in the agreed way • talk about what they have done and found out, e.g. my arm measurement is a bit longer than my foot • engage with other children's explanations and begin to compare approaches	• respond to questions such as 'Of the people you measured, whose foot was about the same length as their arm from elbow to wrist?', 'Do you think it could be true for other people? How could you find out?'

Extension and related activities

Pose 'What if ...?' questions for the children and invite them to change the activity for themselves or others to try on a different occasion. Further activities include:

- Try the test for a different age group.
- Try the test for children that are all a similar height.
- Choose other measurements to compare, e.g. hand span and foot length.

Task: Pathway puzzle

Look at this pathway using 20 squares.

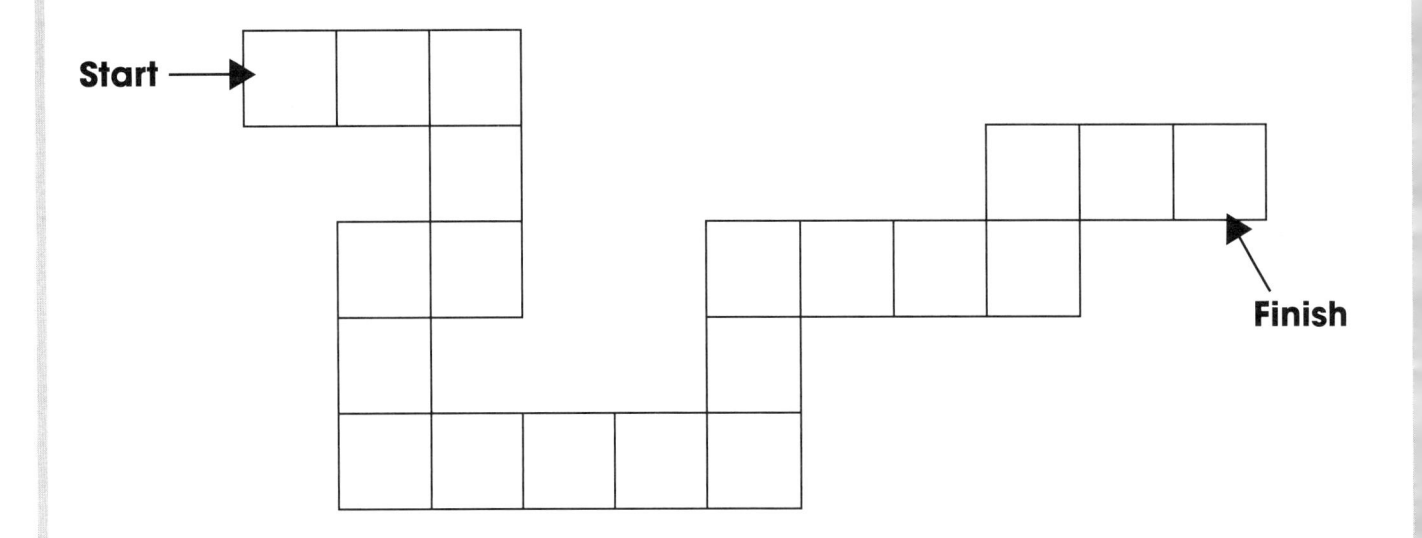

Start → [pathway diagram] **Finish**

Make your own pathway using 20 squares and give a robot or friend instructions to travel along it.

Think about

- Which words do you know to talk about moves, turns and directions?
- How many instructions do you need to give your robot or friend to travel from the start to the finish?

Your task

- Find the pathways using 20 squares that need the least number of instructions and the most.

For the puzzle book

- Write your list of instructions. Challenge people to draw your pathway.

YEAR 3

TASK: PATHWAY PUZZLE

TEACHER NOTES

Framework: Year 3 Block D: Calculating, measuring and understanding shape
Units 1 and 2: Read and record the vocabulary of position, direction and movement using the four compass directions to describe movement about a grid

Materials

- Have a range of materials from which children can make their own selection:
  - square pieces of paper/card/fabric, including large squares to lay out on the floor
  - chalk to draw squares
  - squared paper, e.g. with 5 cm squares
  - scissors
  - small figures/counters that could be moved around smaller pathways
  - robots (if available).

Getting started

- Ask the children how they might get started.
- Leave as many decisions as possible to individual children:
  - how to lay out the pathways
  - whether to use large pathways and larger equipment or smaller pathways and counters
  - the vocabulary for the instructions (e.g. compass directions, quarter turns, right angles, right/left, clockwise/anti-clockwise).
- Check that the children have a way of getting started:
  - you might set out a pathway on the floor and ask one or two children to give instructions for moving round a section of it.

What might happen during the task

- Children make decisions about the shape of their pathway.
- They decide for themselves how to record the pathways and their instructions:
  - drawing the pathways and listing the instructions
  - writing the instructions on the diagram.
- They may be systematic in the way they design the pathways:
  - start with a pathway that needs one instruction to get from the start to the finish and increase the number of instructions by one at a time
  - keep increasing the number of instructions by increasing the number of turns in the pathway.
- They decide whether they have found the shortest and longest list of instructions and demonstrate different degrees of mathematical reasoning:
  - that must be the longest because I can't make it any more
  - I compared my answer to everyone's in the group and no one had a different answer
  - I can't put any more turns in the pathway so that is the greatest number of instructions.
- If a child is stuck, you might ask a question or prompt them to review what they have done so far:
  - how can you arrange the squares?
  - how can you start moving along your pathway?
  - which pathways took more instructions and why?
- Encourage the children to draw conclusions from their activity by talking or writing about what they have found.

What to look for

- Look for what children say and do, as well as what they record.
- Ask questions about the work to gain insights into their thinking.

TASK: PATHWAY PUZZLE

YEAR **3**

ASSESSMENT GUIDANCE

Use the table below to relate the mathematics children demonstrate to assessment focuses and National Curriculum levels.

PROBLEM SOLVING	COMMUNICATING	REASONING
Typically children working at level 3 might:		
• decide which materials to use to set out a pathway and how to give instructions • begin to be systematic, e.g. after some trials, set out to create a pathway that requires only one instruction: Move forwards 20 squares. • review different pathways and recognise that the number of turns determines the number of instructions required	• leave pathways in position as a record or begin to record pathways on paper or using ICT • talk about moves and turns using precise language such as 'forward one (step/unit)', 'quarter turn', 'right angle', 'left/right', 'clockwise', 'anti-clockwise' • make lists of instructions to move from start to finish	• distinguish between straight and turning movements in giving instructions • recognise that each change of direction increases the number of instructions • conclude that a straight pathway requires the least number of instructions and that a zig-zag pathway that changes direction after each 'forward one square' movement has the greatest number
Typically children working at level 2 might:		
• agree which materials to use to set out pathways and an approach to giving instructions • engage with the task in a practical way, e.g. position 20 square cards in a random way to create an interesting pathway and then work out the instructions to give • try different pathways to see if they take the same number of instructions, more or fewer	• leave cards in position as a record of a pathway • speak one instruction at a time to a friend or enter single instructions on the robot's keypad, and after the move, use the new position to work out the next instruction; count the instructions as they are given • begin to record a complete list of instructions for the whole of a pathway	• explain the pathways they created and how many instructions were needed to move from start to finish on each of them • perhaps with the support of probing questions, recognise that pathways with more turns need a greater number of instructions

Extension and related activities

Pose 'What if ...?' questions for the children and invite them to change the activity for themselves or others to try on a different occasion. Further activities include:

- Make a pathway that takes exactly 10 instructions.
- Match pathways to sets of instructions.
- Use playground grids or PE equipment to create pathways.

Task: Time teaser

Miss Allan's class made some films that they want to show at their film club. The films take different lengths of time.

25 minutes — DVD Action

quarter of an hour — MUSICAL DVD

20 minutes — Pets DVD

If the film club starts at half-past three, write a timetable for the club.

Think about

- Different orders to show the films.
- How to work out the start and finish times for each of the films.

Your task

- Write as many different timetables as you can, making sure the start time of each film is correct.

For the puzzle book

- List the films and how long they take. Then make a copy of one of your timetables but leave the names of the films covered. Challenge people to write the names of the films in the order you planned in your timetable.

© Rising Stars UK Ltd 2009. You may photocopy this page.

TASK: TIME TEASER

YEAR 3

TEACHER NOTES

Framework: Year 3 Block D: Calculating, measuring and understanding shape

Units 1 and 3: Read the time on a 12-hour digital clock and to the nearest 5 minutes on an analogue clock; calculate time intervals and find start or end times for a given interval

Materials

- A geared clock
- Non-mechanical card clock faces
- Stamp to print a blank clock face

Getting started

- Ask the children how they might get started.
- Leave as many decisions as possible to individual children:
  - which film to start with
  - whether to allow a change-over time between the films.
- Check that the children have a way of getting started:
  - you might ask one or two children to suggest a film to start with and the time it would finish.

What might happen during the task

- Children make decisions about the order of the films and how to work out the times.
- They decide for themselves how to record their timetables:
  - writing lists
  - using a table.
- They may be systematic in the way they find the timetables:
  - first, find all the timetables that start with Action.
- They decide whether they have found all the timetables and demonstrate different degrees of mathematical reasoning:
  - that is all there are because I can't make any more
  - I compared my timetables to everyone's in the group and no one had a different answer

  - I tried each film as the first film and I can't find any other ways.
- They talk about how they know their time calculations are correct and demonstrate different degrees of mathematical reasoning:
  - I used the geared clock face to help me work them all out
  - I checked my answers
  - all of my timetables give the same finish time for the club so the times must be correct.
- If a child is stuck, you might ask a question or prompt them to review what they have done so far:
  - which film could you show first?
  - how can you work out what time that film will finish?
- Encourage the children to draw conclusions from their activity by talking or writing about what they have found.

What to look for

- Look for what children say and do, as well as what they record.
- Ask questions about the work to gain insights into their thinking.

YEAR 3

TASK: TIME TEASER

ASSESSMENT GUIDANCE

Use the table below to relate the mathematics children demonstrate to assessment focuses and National Curriculum levels.

PROBLEM SOLVING	COMMUNICATING	REASONING
Typically children working at level 3 might:		
• use discussion to clarify the task • decide on ways to generate different orders for showing films and begin to use a systematic approach • compare results, check they have them all and none are repeated • use an analogue clock face to support their thinking in finding start and finish times for each film	• use a list or table to record their timetables • record times in words, e.g. half-past three • begin to use figures to record 12-hour clock times, e.g. 3.45 p.m. • explain how they know they have all possible orders for the films	• begin to use pattern in results, e.g. I found two that started with Action, because it could have Musical then Pets or Pets then Musical …; then two starting with Musical … • review their work to respond to questions such as 'Are the finish times the same for each timetable? Why?'
Typically children working at level 2 might:		
• through discussion, agree an approach to finding different orders in which to show films, e.g. write the names on cards that they can place in order • find different orders to show the films • use a geared analogue clock to work out start and finish times for individual films, e.g. starting with hands showing 3.30, advance the minute hand an appropriate number of minutes forward to show the end time for the first film	• talk about the orders they have found • leave cards with film names on display or record the list so that they can use the same cards again • print a blank clock face and draw hands to show the start time for each film in a timetable • read the time on some if not all of their clock faces	• talk about what is the same and what is different about each timetable they have recorded, e.g. the same films in a different order • talk about how they found different orders to show films, how they know they are different and how they know they have all possible orders

Extension and related activities

Pose 'What if …?' questions for the children and invite them to change the activity for themselves or others to try on a different occasion. Further activities include:

- Put a fourth film into the programme for the club and work out how many different timetables could be made.
- Make a timetable for an evening's programmes on the TV/at the cinema.
- Work out the length of each lesson from the school timetable.
- Use simple bus or train timetables to work out journey times.

Task: Sentence seekers

Find as many ways as you can to complete this number sentence:

20 ÷ ☐ = ☐

How many ways are there to make this sentence correct?

Is there a start number that gives more correct sentences?

Is there a start number that gives fewer correct sentences?

Think about
- Which types of calculation will help you solve this puzzle?

Your task
- Find the start numbers that will give the greatest and least number of sentences.

For the puzzle book
- Write some of the number sentences you have made but miss out one of the numbers. Challenge people to work out the missing numbers.

YEAR 3

TASK: SENTENCE SEEKERS

TEACHER NOTES

Framework: Year 3 Block E: Securing number facts, relationships and calculating
Units 1, 2 and 3: Use practical and informal written methods to multiply and divide two-digit numbers (e.g. 13 × 3, 50 ÷ 4); round remainders up or down, depending on the context
Derive and recall multiplication facts for the 2, 3, 4, 5, 6 and 10 times tables and the corresponding division facts; recognise multiples of 2, 5 or 10 up to 1000

Materials
- Counters
- Calculators

Getting started
- Ask the children how they might get started.
- Leave as many decisions as possible to individual children:
  - which materials or apparatus to use to support their thinking about the problem
  - the range of start numbers to use
  - whether answers must be whole numbers.
- Check that the children have a way of getting started:
  - you might ask one or two children to suggest a way to complete the number sentence on the task sheet.

What might happen during the task
- Children make decisions about which start numbers to use.
- They decide for themselves how to record their work:
  - lists of completed number sentences
  - drawings of 20 counters grouped in various ways to demonstrate solutions
  - tables of results.
- They may be systematic in the way they investigate different numbers:
  - start from one as the divisor and work up
  - use starting numbers from one upwards.
- They decide whether they have found the number with the fewest sentences and demonstrate different degrees of mathematical reasoning:
  - I can't find one with fewer ways
  - these numbers only have two
  - two is the smallest number of ways: you have divide by one or divide by the number itself
  - 1 ÷ 1 = 1 has only one way unless you use fractions.
- They decide whether they have found the number with the most sentences and demonstrate different degrees of mathematical reasoning:
  - no one in the group had a number with more sentences
  - that number will have most because it is in most multiplication tables
  - I could find more if I used fractions.
- If a child is stuck, you might ask a question or prompt them to review what they have done so far:
  - which number could you try to divide it by first?
  - which number haven't you tried yet?
- Encourage the children to draw conclusions from their activity by talking or writing about what they have found.

What to look for
- Look for what children say and do, as well as what they record.
- Ask questions about the work to gain insights into their thinking.

39

TASK: SENTENCE SEEKERS

YEAR 3

ASSESSMENT GUIDANCE

Use the table below to relate the mathematics children demonstrate to assessment focuses and National Curriculum levels.

PROBLEM SOLVING	COMMUNICATING	REASONING
Typically children working at level 3 might:		
• through group discussion, decide on an approach to the problem • use knowledge of halving and doubling or multiplication facts to find some solutions • begin to work or check in a systematic way, e.g. check whether 20 divides exactly by 1, 2, 3, 4 …	• talk about the solutions they find • record results as division sentences	• recognise that multiplication facts provide solutions • notice that results can be paired, e.g. 20 ÷ 2 = 10 and 20 ÷ 10 = 2 • with the support of probing questions, conclude that for any starting number (dividend) there are always two solutions, e.g. 23 ÷ 1 = 23 and 23 ÷ 23 = 1 • talk about the kinds of starting numbers that give rise to many solutions
Typically children working at level 2 might:		
• with the support of discussion, adopt an agreed approach to the problem • use their understanding of division as sharing equally to experiment placing 20 objects into different numbers of groups	• talk about their groupings of 20 counters • begin to read division sentences, e.g. '20 shared by 2 equals 10 each'	• talk about how their grouping of 20 objects relates to the written division sentence • with the support of probing questions, recognise that results can be paired, e.g. 20 ÷ 2 = 10 and 20 ÷ 10 = 2

Extension and related activities

Pose 'What if …?' questions for the children and invite them to change the activity for themselves or others to try on a different occasion. Further activities include:

- Change this problem to make it harder. Then change it to make it easier.
- Use a two-digit start number that isn't in one of your multiplication tables.
- Investigate number sentences with a different operation.

Task: Animal magic!

A magician makes spells using:

bats (2 legs)

spiders (8 legs)

lizards (4 legs)

He needs 24 legs in his magic bag to make a spell.
Can you find some 24-leg spells for the magician?

Think about
- All the different ways there are to get 24 legs with these animals!

Your task
- Find as many different spells using 24 legs as possible for the magician.

For the puzzle book
- Invent and draw some other creatures for the magician to use – perhaps an animal with three legs or with five legs! Challenge people to make spells with 30 legs using the animals you have invented.

© Rising Stars UK Ltd 2009. You may photocopy this page.

TASK: ANIMAL MAGIC! YEAR 3

TEACHER NOTES

Framework: Year 3 Block E: Securing number facts, relationships and calculating
Units 2 and 3: Solve one-step and two-step problems involving numbers, money or measures, including time, choosing and carrying out appropriate calculations

Materials
- Linking cubes or counters

Getting started
- Ask the children how they might get started.
- Leave as many decisions as possible to individual children:
  - whether the order of adding animals creates a different spell.
- Check that the children have a way of getting started:
  - you might ask the children to suggest the first spell.

What might happen during the task
- Children make decisions about which combinations of animals to use.
- They decide for themselves how to record their work:
  - drawing the animals
  - drawing symbols for the animals
  - writing lists
  - making tables.
- They may be systematic in the way they investigate the spells:
  - find all the spells with just one type of animal, then two, then three
  - find all the spells with three spiders, then two spiders, then one …
- They decide whether they have found all the possible spells and demonstrate different degrees of mathematical reasoning:
  - I can't find any more
  - I have used all the animals so that is all there are
  - I compared my spells to everyone's in the group and no one had any others
  - I found all the spells with spiders, then the spells with just lizards and bats, and then the spells with just bats.
- If a child is stuck, you might ask a question or prompt them to review what they have done so far:
  - which animals have you used?
  - do you need to use all the animals every time?
  - which animal could you try using just one of?
- Encourage the children to draw conclusions from their activity by talking or writing about what they have found.

What to look for
- Look for what children say and do, as well as what they record.
- Ask questions about the work to gain insights into their thinking.

YEAR 3

TASK: ANIMAL MAGIC!

ASSESSMENT GUIDANCE

Use the table below to relate the mathematics children demonstrate to assessment focuses and National Curriculum levels.

PROBLEM SOLVING	COMMUNICATING	REASONING
Typically children working at level 3 might:		
• use discussion to engage with the investigation • decide how to represent the different animals, e.g. use cube animals, drawings, number cards • decide how to record spells • begin to work in a systematic way, e.g. look for all the spells that have only one type of animal, two types of animal etc. • compare results with a partner and recognise which are the same or different • check for repeats	• record spells in a list or table • begin to refine their recording to be less time-consuming if necessary, e.g. stop drawing animals and just record the number of each type or the number of legs, e.g. 4 + 4 + 4 + 4 + 4 + 4 to represent six lizards	• begin to use pattern in results to check they have all possible spells • respond to questions such as 'What would happen if he could also use beetles with six legs?', 'Could he use just beetles? Just beetles and spiders?'
Typically children working at level 2 might:		
• through discussion, agree how to represent the animals, e.g. use linking cubes and link two blue cubes to represent a bat, link four green cubes to represent a lizard etc. • put collections of 'animals' together, counting the legs (cubes) until there are 24 • through discussion, agree what 'different spells' means, e.g. the same animals in a different order does not count as a different spell	• talk about the collections of animals they have made • leave the cube 'animals' in sets to demonstrate possible spells • with support, put the animals in each set into order starting with those that have most legs to check for repeats	• talk about what is the same and what is different about their collections, e.g. these spells both have two spiders but they have different animals for the rest of the legs • with support, identify repeats • talk about the number of different spells they have made

Extension and related activities

Pose 'What if ...?' questions for the children and invite them to change the activity for themselves or others to try on a different occasion. Further activities include:

- Use a different choice of animals.
- Invent animals with unlikely numbers of legs.
- Use in the context of animals in a cave or other habitat.

Name .... Class .... Date ....

My progress and targets

Tick the circles to show what you do when you solve problems or investigate in mathematics.

PROBLEM SOLVING	COMMUNICATING	REASONING
○ When we talk about a problem, I understand what it is about and decide how to get started	○ I talk about my work and use mathematical words to explain it	○ I explain what we had to do, how I decided to work and my results
○ I decide for myself what apparatus or materials to use	○ I record my work using drawings, words, number sentences, tables, sorting diagrams and graphs	○ I read the number sentences I write and explain what my diagrams and graphs show
○ I check how my work is going and try a different way if I need to	○ Sometimes I group my results or put them into order to help me check them	○ When my teacher makes a statement, I can find examples in my work to show if it is true or not
○ I listen to my teacher and talk with children in my group so that I know what we have to do	○ I talk about how I am doing my work and sometimes I use the mathematical words we have been learning	○ When I look at my work, I can talk about how I worked things out
○ When my teacher talks about different apparatus we could use, I decide what I shall use	○ I use apparatus to show what I am doing	○ I explain how I know my work is right
○ I think about how to record my work so that I remember what I have done	○ I record my work in different ways – pictures and words – number sentences – diagrams and graphs	○ I talk about how some results are the same or how they are different

✎ Now write out targets on a separate piece of paper for when you do activities like this again.

'When I solve problems and investigate again, I will try to …'

YEAR 3

SOLUTIONS

Page 8 - 'V'ery puzzling

There are three basic solutions:

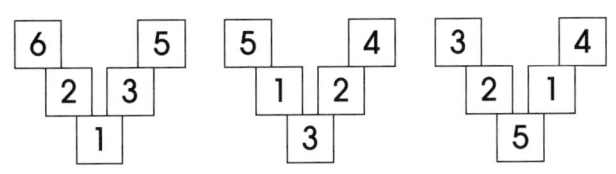

```
 6     5       5     4       3     4
  2 3           1 2           2 1
   1             3             5
```

Children may include arrangements where cards on the edges of the 'V' are the same as above but ordered differently. The first solution above can be rearranged in three more ways:

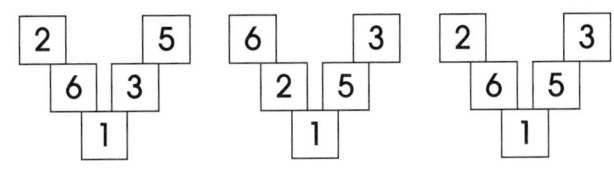

```
 2     5       6     3       2     3
  6 3           2 5           6 5
   1             1             1
```

If all three basic solutions are rearranged in these ways, there are a total of 12 solutions, including the basic ones.

Additionally, children may include reflections of 12 solutions:

```
 6     3              3     6
  2 5        →         5 2
   1                    1
```

If all reflections are included, there are 24 solutions.

Page 11 - Blank puzzles

For the two-digit totals:

9 + 3 = 12   8 + 2 = 10   7 + 3 = 10   6 + 4 = 10
9 + 4 = 13   8 + 4 = 12   7 + 5 = 12
9 + 5 = 14   8 + 5 = 13   7 + 6 = 13
9 + 6 = 15   8 + 6 = 14
9 + 7 = 16   8 + 7 = 15
9 + 8 = 17

Recording the largest single-digit number first, there are 15 possible solutions, shown above.

Children may add the same pair of single-digit numbers in the reverse order:

9 + 3 = 12 and 3 + 9 = 12

If they do, there are 30 possible solutions.

If children choose to allow zero as a place holder in the tens position of the two-digit number, many more solutions are possible, e.g. 1 + 2 = 03

For the three-digit totals:

4 + 98 = 102   5 + 97 = 102   7 + 96 = 103   7 + 95 = 102   8 + 94 = 102
5 + 98 = 103   6 + 97 = 103   8 + 96 = 104   8 + 95 = 103
6 + 98 = 104   8 + 97 = 105
7 + 98 = 105

If children choose to use zero as a place holder in the hundreds position of the three-digit number, many more solutions are possible, e.g. 5 + 86 = 091

45

SOLUTIONS

YEAR 3

Page 14 – Jump to it!
Isaac's sequences that include 20 are:

0, 1, 2, 3, 4, 5, 6, 7, 8, 9, 10, 11, 12, 13, 14, 15, 16, 17, 18, 19, 20 …
0, 2, 4, 6, 8, 10, 12, 14, 16, 18, 20 …
0, 4, 8, 12, 16, 20 …
0, 5, 10, 15, 20 …
0, 10, 20 …

Each of the sequences above, apart from the third, can be extended to include 20 and 50 as well. There are no other sequences of whole numbers that start at 0 and include both 20 and 50. If children decide to try sequences that do not start at 0 but do include both 20 and 50, there are:

start at 2 and make jumps of six: 2, 8, 14, 20, 26, 32, 38, 44, 50 …
start at 5 and make jumps of 15: 5, 20, 35, 50 …

Page 17 – Be square

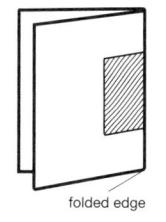

Children may cut around three edges of a rectangle that is twice as long on the folded edge of the paper as it is wide

The other way to create a square involves cutting around two edges of a triangle, like this: an isosceles, right-angled triangle. The cut edges are equal in length.

Page 20 – Reflect on this
Symmetrical shapes that can be made are:

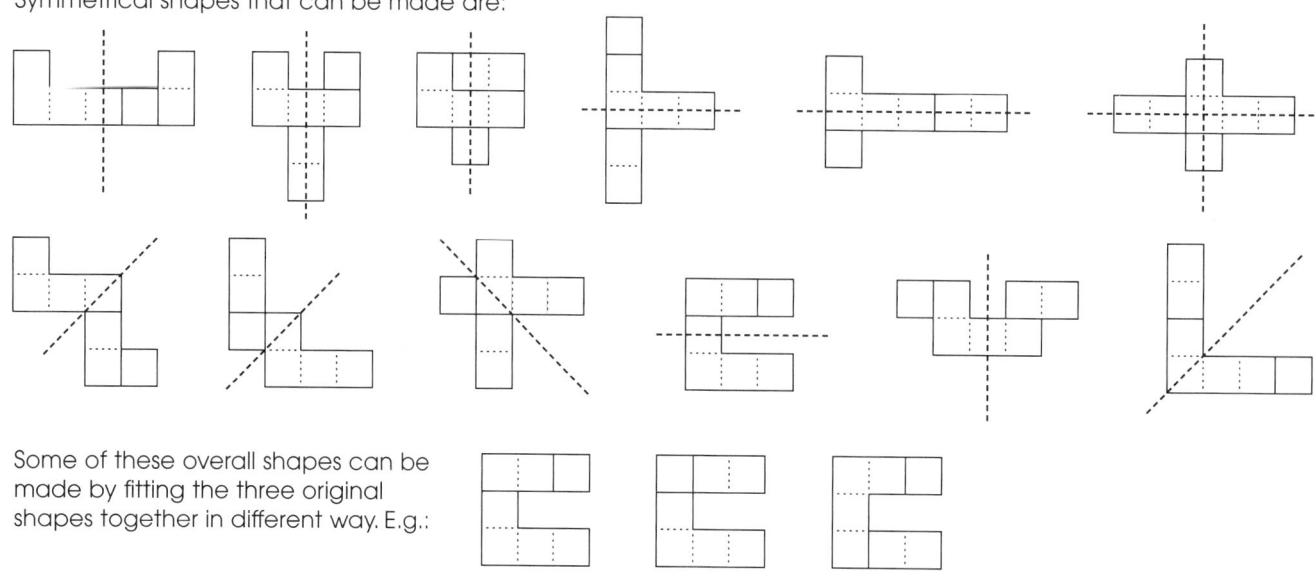

Some of these overall shapes can be made by fitting the three original shapes together in different way. E.g.:

Page 23 – A right 't'angle
Solutions include:

Quadrilaterals with no right angles:

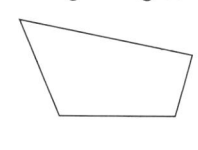

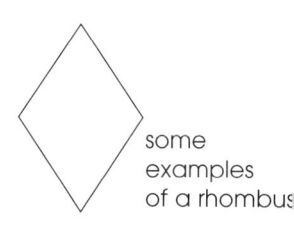

parallelogram

some examples of a kite

some examples of a rhombus

Quadrilaterals with one right angle:

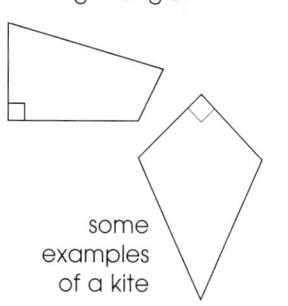

Quadrilaterals with two right angles:

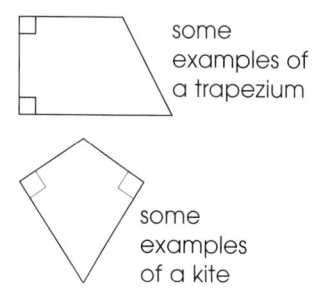

some examples of a trapezium

There are no quadrilaterals with exactly three right angles.

Quadrilaterals with four right angles:

'oblong' rectangle

square

some examples of a kite

some examples of a kite

YEAR 3

SOLUTIONS

Page 26 – The YES – NO puzzle

Sorting numbers 1–30 into the Carroll diagram:

	multiples of 3	not multiples of 3
multiples of 2	6, 12, 18, 24, 30	2, 4, 8, 10, 14, 16, 20, 22, 26, 28
not multiples of 2	3, 9, 15, 21, 27	1, 5, 7, 11, 13, 17, 19, 23, 25, 29

Children might include numbers greater than 30.

They might notice that numbers that are multiples of 2 *and* multiples of 3 are the multiples of 6.

They might talk about the parts of the diagram that have even numbers or odd numbers.

Page 29 – Put your foot down!

In using and applying their mathematics, children make decisions for themselves about how to undertake an investigation or solve a problem. They respond in different ways. Given the wide range of possible responses, this task does not have a 'solution'. The Teacher notes and Assessment guidance for this task explain what you might observe, how children might record their data, and the types of conclusions that children might draw from their activity.

Page 32 – Pathway puzzle

A straight line of squares requires the least number of instructions:
'move forwards 20 squares'.

A pathway that involves moving only one square before changing direction requires the greatest number of instructions:

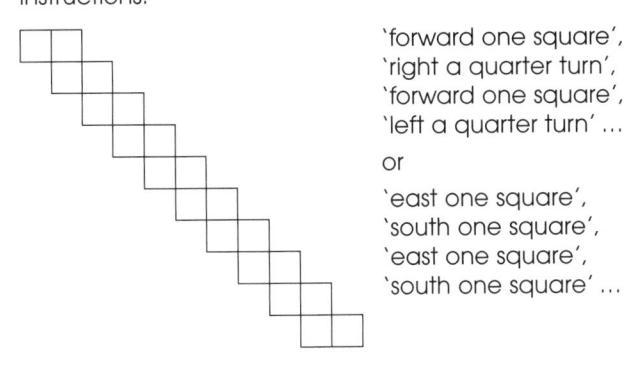

'forward one square',
'right a quarter turn',
'forward one square',
'left a quarter turn' …

or

'east one square',
'south one square',
'east one square',
'south one square' …

Page 35 – Time teaser

There are six different orders for showing the three films. (These solutions do not include an interval or separate change-over times.)

3.30 Action	3.30 Action	3.30 Musical	3.30 Musical	3.30 Pets	3.30 Pets
3.55 Musical	3.55 Pets	3.45 Action	3.45 Pets	3.50 Action	3.50 Musical
4.10 Pets	4.15 Musical	4.10 Pets	4.05 Action	4.15 Musical	4.05 Action
4.30 Finish	4.30 Finish	4.30 Finish	4.30 Finish	4.30 Finish	4.30 Finish

SOLUTIONS

YEAR 3

Page 38 - Sentence seekers

For the example given on the task sheet:

20 ÷ 1 = 20
20 ÷ 2 = 10
20 ÷ 4 = 5
20 ÷ 5 = 4
20 ÷ 10 = 2
20 ÷ 20 = 1

Start numbers that give the least number of sentences include 1 and then prime numbers, e.g.:

1 ÷ 1 = 1	2 ÷ 1 = 2	3 ÷ 1 = 3	5 ÷ 1 = 5	7 ÷ 1 = 7
	2 ÷ 2 = 1	3 ÷ 3 = 1	5 ÷ 5 = 1	7 ÷ 7 = 1

Start numbers that give many sentences have many factors and include:

24 ÷ 1 = 24	36 ÷ 1 = 36	48 ÷ 1 = 48	60 ÷ 1 = 60
24 ÷ 2 = 12	36 ÷ 2 = 18	48 ÷ 2 = 24	60 ÷ 2 = 30
24 ÷ 3 = 8	36 ÷ 3 = 12	48 ÷ 3 = 16	60 ÷ 3 = 20
24 ÷ 4 = 6	36 ÷ 4 = 9	48 ÷ 4 = 12	60 ÷ 4 = 15
24 ÷ 6 = 4	36 ÷ 6 = 6	48 ÷ 6 = 8	60 ÷ 5 = 12
24 ÷ 8 = 3	36 ÷ 9 = 4	48 ÷ 8 = 6	60 ÷ 6 = 10
24 ÷ 12 = 2	36 ÷ 12 = 3	48 ÷ 12 = 4	60 ÷ 10 = 6
24 ÷ 24 = 1	36 ÷ 18 = 2	48 ÷ 16 = 3	60 ÷ 12 = 5
	36 ÷ 36 = 1	48 ÷ 24 = 2	60 ÷ 15 = 4
		48 ÷ 48 = 1	60 ÷ 20 = 3
			60 ÷ 30 = 2
			60 ÷ 60 = 1

Page 41 - Animal magic!

Spiders (8 legs)	Lizards (4 legs)	Bats (2 legs)	Total number of legs
3	0	0	24
2	2	0	24
2	1	2	24
2	0	4	24
1	4	0	24
1	3	2	24
1	2	4	24
1	1	6	24
1	0	8	24
0	6	0	24
0	5	2	24
0	4	4	24
0	3	6	24
0	2	8	24
0	1	10	24
0	0	12	24

There are 16 possible spells with 24 legs.